The World of
Freshwater Fish

The World of
Freshwater Fish

Thomas D. Fegely

Illustrated with photographs and drawings

DODD, MEAD & COMPANY • New York

ILLUSTRATION CREDITS

Allentown *Call-Chronicle* Newspapers, 32, 58 (by Larry Vadelund); Ben Callaway, 64; Mike Markowitz, 11, 12, 13, 21 (left); David Miller, 52; National
Aquarium, 121; Pennsylvania Fish Commission, 22, 23 (by Russ Gettig), 24,
25, 27 (top), 95, 102, 122; Rapala Lure Company, 62; Leonard Lee Rue III,
42; Tennessee Conservation Department, 83; U.S. Fish and Wildlife Service,
71, 82 (by Bob Hines), 92, 101, 105, 114, and 115. All other photographs are
by Thomas D. Fegely.

26704

1 2 3 4 5 6 7 8 9 10

Library of Congress Cataloging in Publication Data

Fegely, Thomas D.
The world of freshwater fish.

Bibliography: p. 125
Includes index.
SUMMARY: Discusses the physical characteristics,
habits, and natural environment of a variety of freshwater fish found on the North American continent.
  1.   Fishes, Freshwater—Juvenile literature.
  2.   Fishes—North America—Juvenile literature.
[1.   Fishes, Freshwater.   2.   Fishes—North America]
I.   Title.
QL617.2.F43   597'.0929   77–16879
ISBN 0–396–07562–2

To Betty Ann and Charlie

Contents

Over 800 different kinds of freshwater fish live in North America.

1. North America's Freshwater Fish

Over 800 different kinds of freshwater fish swim in the lakes, rivers, and streams across the North American continent. Each has a particular habitat in which to live, reproduce, and die.

Some, like the trout, prefer cold, oxygen-rich waters, churning and tumbling down tree-lined streams. The pike family prowls weed-infested backwaters of lakes and rivers for unsuspecting minnows and frogs. Catfish grow fat on the bottom of warm, slow-moving rivers, and whitefish patrol the blackened lake bottom 200 yards below the surface.

A few species of fish dwell in both fresh water and salt water at some time in their lives. Some feed exclusively on insects and others devour practically anything that moves and is small enough to be swallowed. A few even eat their own young.

Although it is impossible for scientists to tell how many different species of fish there actually are, recent estimates place the world's total at about 21,500 different kinds. Of these, about 4,000 species inhabit North American waters—salt, brackish, and fresh. About 20 percent of these fish live in fresh water at one time or another in their lives.

The secluded watery homes of fish seldom allow us to peek in on their daily lives as we do squirrels and rabbits or robins and insects.

Game fish and panfish are popular with fishermen. Here a yellow perch (top), smallmouth bass (rear), and a walleye swim together.

Freshwater fish exist in a variety of sizes from tiny fry that weigh only a fraction of an ounce to giants that tip the scales at a thousand pounds or more.

Within the past century man has become conscious of the vast potential for food and recreation offered by our freshwater fish, and many millions of dollars have been spent in maintaining and managing them. This has resulted in freshwater species being shipped from all over the United States and abroad to eventually inhabit streams and lakes far from their native waters.

The wonders of freshwater fish are many and varied. Because of their great varieties and the many types of habitats in which they live, freshwater fish exist within walking distance of practically every American and provide countless hours of relaxation through the sport of angling.

2. The Freshwater Fish—
Inside and Out

In outward appearance, most fish look somewhat alike. That is not to say that we cannot separate a bluegill from a perch or a trout from a bass, but upon close study one will plainly see that all fish possess the same basic body parts. The illustration below shows the names of the various fins and other parts referred to throughout this book.

A fish's internal characteristics are really much the same as

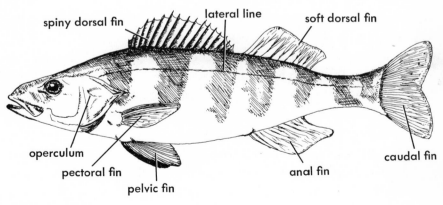

External features

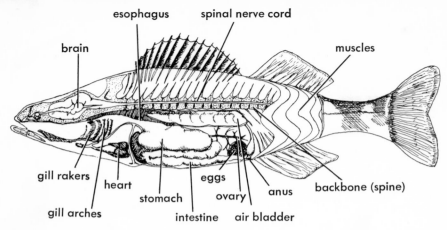

esophagus spinal nerve cord

brain

muscles

gill rakers

heart

eggs

stomach

ovary

anus

backbone (spine)

gill arches

intestine   air bladder

Internal features

man's. Both have skeletons, muscles, a heart and circulatory system, a brain and nervous system, a digestive system with an esophagus, stomach, and intestines, and a system to remove body wastes. The two big differences are in the methods of respiration and the possession of an air bladder in most fish.

As water is taken in through a fish's mouth, it is strained through a set of *gill rakers*, then it passes between *gill arches*, over the gills, and back out of its body through *operculums*.

The gills are located beneath the operculums (which protect them) on each side of the head. The gills are supplied with a vast network of blood vessels very close to the surface. This is why a fish's gills appear bright red and should be kept from injury when a fish is caught and returned to the water. As oxygen-rich water passes over the gills, the oxygen *diffuses* (passes into the bloodstream where there is less oxygen) into the fish's body. Carbon dioxide, the fish's waste gas, passes from the blood into the water in a reverse manner.

A fish's *air bladder* seems to have two functions. Most importantly, it serves as a balance organ and a device for adjusting the depths at which a fish can swim. For example, have you ever tried to pull an inflatable toy below the surface of the water while swimming? If so, you probably noticed that a toy filled with air is much more difficult to submerge than one with very little air in it. A fish can control the amount of air in its air bladder and thereby choose the depth in which it wants to swim. The less air it contains in the bladder, the deeper it can go. Fish without air (or gas) bladders must be constantly on the move to keep from sinking.

Ichthyologists (scientists who study fish) have also determined that some fish use their air bladders as hearing aids and and as vibrators for sending out noises. As vibrations pass through the water, they are detected by a fish's air-filled bladder. A few fish can give off grunts and groans by expanding and contracting the air bladder—thereby communicating to others elsewhere in a dark lake or river.

One feature which ties all fish to one another is that they are covered with *scales*. These scales are embedded in the inner layer of skin and vary from thumbnail size or larger down to microscopic size. Freshwater fish may possess any of three scale types known as *ganoid, ctenoid,* or *cycloid* scales. *Ganoid* scales are possessed by a few primitive bony fishes such as the gars.

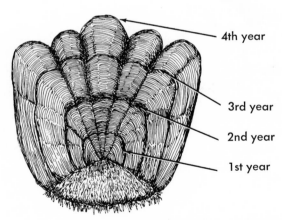

4th year

3rd year

2nd year

1st year

As a fish grows, its scales do not increase in number, but they do increase in size. In summer when food is available, the scales grow fast. In winter growth slows, and the dark rings appear—just like that of a tree.

13

Some of the primitive fish, such as this gar, possess ganoid scales.

These scales are diamond-shaped and attached to each other by joints. They are coated with a substance that gives the fish the appearance of being "polished."

Ctenoid scales have a comblike edge, while *cycloid* scales have a rounded border. Most freshwater fish have one or the other of these two scale types. As the scales grow, they form rings similar to the annual growth rings of a tree.

In winter the growth of these scales is usually slower than during the warmer summer months. This slower growth causes the rings to grow closer together, forming an "annual ring." In some fish, counting the number of these annual rings will tell you the fish's age.

3. How Does a Fish . . . .

BREATHE?

As explained, a fish breathes by use of its blood vessel-rich gills. Some fish even use atmospheric air when the water supply of oxygen falls short. For example, carp that dwell in ponds or shallow lakes often run short of oxygen during the warm summer months. In warm water all fish require more oxygen than they do in winter because their body processes speed up. Carp

Fish get their oxygen directly from the water by creating a current over their blood vessel-rich gills. Note the bits of fine gravel dropping from this carp's operculum as it feeds on the bottom.

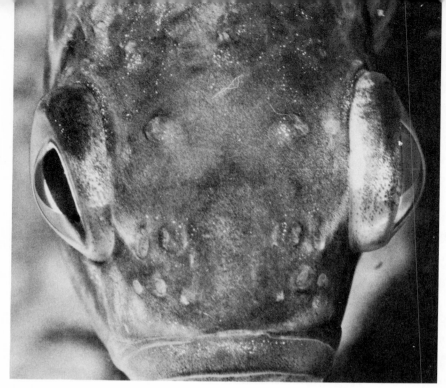

A fish's eyes are spherical and rigid.

often live in sluggish water where there is little available oxygen. When this happens, it merely gulps a bubble of air which is held in its mouth near the moist gills to supply the needed oxygen. Some of the ancient freshwater fishes, such as the gar and the bowfin, still possess a primitive lung which serves them in time of air shortage. This "lung" developed into the gas bladder in most fish but never did so in the ones that existed millions of years ago and managed to survive to modern times.

See?

The eyes of fish are similar to those of land animals in many respects. There are a few major differences, though, that result from daily living in an underwater world.

One important difference results from the absence of brilliant light in most underwater situations. This enables a fish to get along with little or no contraction of the iris. In most fish, the iris does not have the ability to move at all, since it is never necessary to regulate the amount of light passing into the eye.

Fish can also get along without eyelids, since their watery environment continually washes their eyes and keeps them free of the many dust particles that affect the eyes of terrestrial creatures. When a fish sleeps, as some do, the eyes tend to lose their abilities to see, much the same as ours do when they are shut.

At its very best, underwater vision seems to be limited to less than 35 yards. Most fish, therefore, need only focus on nearby objects. Hence, nature has designed their eyes to be spherical and rigid, not rounded and flexible like ours.

The one advantage fish have over humans in the way of sight is that they can see in more than one direction at a time. They have what is known as *monocular* vision (only using one eye at a time), since the eyes are located at the sides of the head rather than up front. There is reason to believe, however, that

Fish have monocular vision, which means they can see in more than one direction at a time.

fish do have a narrow area straight ahead in which they do use both eyes and hence have a limited *binocular* vision. This type of vision enables a fish to properly judge distances. Often, when a fish sights a disturbance, it whirls around and faces it straight on where its distance can be better estimated.

It is known that all freshwater fish can, to some degree, see color. Microscopic examination of the nerve cells inside the eyes of fish has revealed the presence of *cones* which are necessary to distinguish colors by all animals. There is much to be learned about the ways in which fish use their ability to distinguish colors. Many fishing-lure manufacturers would like to gain knowledge of the color preferences of different game fish so that irresistible lures could be designed to catch them.

One very special problem encountered by fish, particularly those that take their food from the water's surface, is a condition known as *refraction*. This is the term used to describe the "bending" of light as it passes from air into water. When we look into a pool of water at any angle other than from directly above, the object we are looking at is not actually where it appears to be. Similarly, a trout or bass rising to catch an insect skittering just above the surface of the water must actually strike a short distance ahead of its target. Down through the ages this problem was worked out within the fish's ancestry so that it is now a built-in instinctive skill.

Hear?

Fish can detect vibrations passing through the water, but most biologists agree that they do not really *hear* a sound in the true sense of the word. As previously mentioned, the air bladder serves to record vibrations traveling through the water. Fish, however, do not possess eardrums or the middle ear structure of higher animals.

Even though they can't hear, fish do have "ears." Located in the bones of the skull, these simple ears pick up vibrations from

Fish "hear" with the help of their lateral lines. A magnifying glass shows a lateral line of a brook trout.

throughout the entire body and transmit the information to the brain. It is also known that these crude "ears," with no external openings, serve to aid the fish in maintaining its balance.

An extraordinary "sixth sense" possessed by all freshwater fish may also be linked to the hearing or vibration detection process. The *lateral lines*, readily visible on most fish, are made up of a series of pores along each side of the body. These small pores, or openings, connect to a canal that runs just under the skin's surface. Along this canal are numerous sense organs called *neuromasts*. Inside each neuromast are numerous hairlike structures that vibrate when there is any sort of disturbance in the water. Fish are able to use this lateral line system to pick up low vibrations caused by the movements of other fish, including the larger predators and smaller prey. This is why a fisherman should sneak along the bank of a stream or pond in which he wants to fish. Heavy footsteps will alert any fish lying nearby and the angler is usually detected by the fish long before he is seen.

19

This sturgeon uses its barbels to locate and actually "taste" food before it is eaten.

Taste and Smell?

Some species of fish have excellent senses of taste and smell. Fishes that hunt at night, like eels, catfish, and carp, rely largely on scent to find their foodstuffs. Scientists also believe it is the scent from the stream in which it was hatched that enables a salmon to return to its birthplace after four or five years of life in the sea.

Although most animals have their sense of taste only in their mouths, fish have the ability to taste with cells both in the mouth as well as on the lips, and on special organs known as *barbels*. Catfish, sturgeon, and carp use these barbels to probe the watery environment and can actually "taste" what they are going to eat before getting it in their mouths. They may also be attracted to a food's location or repelled from a polluted pool by this same sense.

Swim?

When a person swims through the water, the hands, arms, and legs are used in a pushing-and-pulling motion. A fish moves through water by a side-to-side movement of the tail which actually "pushes" the fish's body forward. The *caudal*, or tail, fin is, therefore, the most important and powerful of all the fins.

The *dorsal*, or back, fin helps the fish maintain an upright position, and the other fins control balance and steering from right to left. These fins, especially the front or *pectoral* fins, also enable the fish to put on the "brakes" and make quick turns.

A fish swims by moving its tail in a snakelike motion and actually "pushing" its way through the water. A complete body stroke is shown in this diagram, left.

The dorsal fin helps this small largemouth bass, below, maintain an upright position. The pectoral fins enable it to steer and make quick turns or stop abruptly.

A male (front) and female brook trout about to begin spawning in a shallow stony nest constructed by the female.

The female, heavily laden with eggs, begins to spawn. The male will fertilize the eggs with his milt.

Both trout strain to eject the sex cells from their bodies.

REPRODUCE AND GROW?

Baby fish begin life in one of two ways—either by developing from an egg or by being born alive.

As in other animals, a sperm, from a male fish, and an egg, from a female fish, must combine before any life begins. This combination of egg and sperm is called *fertilization*. In land animals it is necessary for the male to fertilize the egg inside the female's body during the mating process. In a water environment, however, the water itself is sometimes used to enable the sperm and the egg to meet.

A brook trout, for example, will dig a shallow nest in a brook in which to deposit her eggs. When she is ready, the eggs are shed into the cleared spot and the male simultaneously releases a cloud of *milt* into the water next to her. The milt contains millions of sperm cells to insure that at least one will be able to fertilize every egg laid. This mating process of fish is known as *spawning*.

Over a period of time ranging from ten to thirty days, depending on the type of fish and water temperatures, the eggs

In a few days, the fertilized eggs hatch into fry.

The fry gets its first nourishment by using up its yolk sac.

As the fish grows, the yolk sac disappears and it begins to feed.

This small trout is surrounded by daphnia—a nutritious food eaten by hatchery-raised trout as well as those hatched in the wild.

Fish grow at varied rates. Would you believe that the 5-inch male brook trout is the same age as the 16-inch hatchery-raised trout above it? It is. The hatchery fish was pampered with an exceptionally rich diet, while the smaller fish, born in the wild, had to find its own food.

will hatch into tiny fish called *fry*. In some species such as catfish, bass, and sticklebacks, the male will stay around to protect the youngsters until they are ready to leave the nest. In others, such as trout, perch, and shad, the parents leave soon after spawning and never see their offspring. The young fish hatch out and are left to fend for themselves.

When a baby fish hatches from the egg, it stays attached to part of the yolk, which gives it nourishment during its first days of life. At this time it swims in short, jerky movements. As the yolk is used up, the swimming ability of the fry becomes better, and soon it travels around with others of its kind, eating small food which it catches itself.

Young fish grow at varying rates, depending on their species and where they live. A rainbow trout grows to 6 inches by its second summer, while it may take a walleye only half that length of time to reach the same size.

4. Fish Behavior

FOOD PREFERENCES AND HABITS

Most freshwater fish familiar to us feed on insects, worms, crayfish, tadpoles, frogs, mollusks, and other fish. Every once in a while a snake, muskrat, or duck is caught and eaten by one of the larger fishes, such as a muskellunge or northern pike.

Of all the things that determine what a fish eats, the most important are the fish's size, swimming speed, habitat, and mouth structure. As a fish grows, from a fry to an adult, its food preferences often change drastically. A chain pickerel, just after hatching, feeds on the microscopic life of a pond. As it grows its diet changes to insects, crayfish, and worms, then other fish (including its own kind).

It is only natural that the largest fish will eat the largest prey. It is not unusual for a 4-foot muskellunge to swallow a young duck or for a largemouth bass to eat a small muskrat.

A muskellunge is equipped with long, pointed teeth, which it uses to catch and hold its prey until it can be swallowed whole. It usually lies in ambush waiting for some unsuspecting fish to pass close by, then swiftly swims after it and grabs it sideways in its mouth.

Trout, on the other hand, patrol the stream floor for insect larvae or lie behind a rock, occasionally swimming out to grab

Above, young muskellunge (bottom) first feed on daphnia (top), then as they grow begin to prey on small suckers (middle).

As the musky matures, its strong, sharp teeth enable it to eat other fish and even ducklings and small mammals.

The largemouth bass is a voracious fish-eater.

a small minnow or bit of food from the water's surface.

Catfish search the floors of their pond or river homes, feeding on a variety of plant and animal life, including those things that are dead.

Aquatic vegetation, fish eggs, terrestrial insects that fall in the water, and even seeds and small fruits are consumed by some fish.

The position and shape of a fish's mouth also help determine the kinds of foods it can eat. A bottom-feeding fish, such as the sturgeon, has its mouth conveniently located on the under-side of the head. The stickleback, a surface-feeder that eats mosquito larvae, has its mouth on the upper side of the head.

The sucker's mouth is equipped with fleshy, tubelike lips, which enable it to take foods from the bottom in a sucking fashion. A largemouth bass can open its mouth wide enough to swallow a baseball. Garfish have long, pointed snouts with

28

The sucker's mouth is equipped with fleshy, tube-like lips, which "vacuum" the stream or river bottom.

large, tooth-studded mouths for catching other fish.

The teeth of large fish are used only for getting a firm hold on their slippery-skinned prey. Many fish possess small *vomerine* teeth on the roof of the mouth to aid in grasping. Some of the members of the minnow and sucker families have special teeth in the throat that aid in crushing plant food and small shelled animals.

Courtship and Mating

Each species of fish has its own special method of attracting a mate, preparing to nest, and actually carrying out the mating or *spawning* process.

The males of some species of minnows become brightly colored as their spring mating season approaches. The redbelly dace, for example, is considered one of the most beautiful and colorful of all fish at this time. Its fins and sides take on shades

29

The male smallmouth bass builds the nest, then guards the eggs and fry. (Note the eggs scattered on the rock.)

Minnows simply school together and shed their eggs and sperm into the water at random at spawning time.

of red, orange, and yellow. The chief reasons for this flashy dress are to attract females and to warn other males that they are trespassing in *his* territory.

Quite often it is the male, not the female, that builds a nest in the stony ripples of a stream or near the bank of a pond or lake. The male smallmouth bass attracts females into the nest where they shed eggs which he immediately fertilizes. The female then leaves and others may come to the nest and the process again takes place. Finally the male smallmouth settles down to the chore of caring for and protecting the eggs and fry until they are ready to leave the nest area.

Some fish do not build nests at all, and for many there is no apparent mating attraction. Certain minnows, males and females both, may simply school together in some quiet area where they release their sex cells (eggs and sperm) into the water. When the process is over, the adults go their own ways and the eggs sink to the bottom. Some of the eggs will hatch into fry, while others may be eaten by predator fish or turtles.

The spawning processes of our freshwater fish are many and varied. As each family or fish is highlighted in later chapters, strange, unusual, and interesting spawning methods will be discussed.

HYBRIDIZATION

Hybridization is defined as the crossing or mating of two different species of animals. The resulting offspring, usually having some characteristics of *each* of the parents, are known as *hybrids*.

Under natural conditions, most species of fish will only mate with others of their kind. There are some exceptions to this, however. Members of the sunfish family frequently mate with other species, and hybrid sunfish are common. For example, the redear sunfish and the green sunfish frequently breed with one

The tiger muskellunge is a hybrid of northern pike-true muskellunge parents.

another, and the hybrids that result are difficult to identify as one or the other.

Man has also had much to do with hybridizing fish to come up with new and faster-growing or more colorful types. The tiger muskellunge is the result of a northern pike-muskellunge mating. The splake results from the mating of brook trout and lake trout.

Quite often the offspring of unlike parents are *sterile*. For example, hybrid tiger "muskies" cannot produce other tiger muskies. The hybrid fish are always offspring of northern pike-muskellunge parents—never tiger muskellunge parents.

MIGRATION

Although we usually associate the word *migration* with birds, some species of fish also migrate. That is, they move from one location to another—usually for the purpose of spawning. The distance covered in such migrations may range from less than a mile up to 2,000 miles or more.

The American shad moves from salt water to fresh water to spawn each spring. Their migrations sometimes cover hundreds of miles. These are the eggs of a female shad.

The most famous migrator of all is surely the Pacific salmon. These fish, after hatching and traveling downstream from their birthplaces to the ocean, are able to return to the exact same spot in which they hatched years earlier. Other fishes, including the shad, American eel, and steelhead trout, carry out similar migration runs which will be detailed later.

Although the longest migrations take place with fish that move from fresh to salt water or vice versa, some fish merely move from lakes and rivers into smaller tributary streams. Anglers refer to these seasonal movements as "runs," and fishing is usually very good at these times. Smelt, suckers, trout, and pike all move from their normal habitats to specialized places for spawning at various times of the year.

In the past, Indians and pioneer settlers took advantage of the massive migration runs of many species of fish to build up their food supplies. Using large nets or simply catching the fish by hand, they welcomed the easy food and gorged themselves on fresh fish. Since there was no refrigeration available at that time, extra fish were either dried in the sun or smoked for use later on.

RESPONSE TO TEMPERATURE

All fish are *cold-blooded* animals. That is, their body temperatures are always the same as the waters in which they swim.

Sensitive cells located along the lateral lines play an important part in enabling a fish to recognize heat and cold. Scientists do not believe that a fish is made uncomfortable by great changes in water temperatures, unless the change is made too quickly. The main effects of great temperature changes, as occur in the extremes of summer and winter, are that the fish's activities and eating habits change. At each of these extremes, fish tend to become sluggish and eat very little. In winter most freshwater fish become partly dormant, and during the hot weeks of summer they move to deeper, cooler water and feed very little. This is

These northern pike have a preferred temperature of 63 degrees and will adjust the depths at which they swim throughout the seasons to find a close temperature.

why fishing always tends to be best in the spring and autumn months when water temperatures are changing.

All fish seem to have "preferred feeding temperatures." That is, they will feed most heavily when the water temperature falls in the range they like best. This "preferred feeding temperature" may be determined by the change of seasons or, for some fish, by simply seeking an area of a lake or deep pond that they find most comfortable.

Modern fishermen, using sophisticated equipment in their boats, locate the various water temperatures of a lake, then concentrate their fishing efforts in those places.

Scientists have studied different species of fish and now know the most desirable feeding temperature of each species. As the water temperature moves away from the preferred temperature, the rate at which a fish feeds tends to drop. Here are the preferred feeding temperatures of some popular game fish.

Channel catfish	72°
Bluegill	69°
Largemouth bass	68°
Yellow perch	68°
Crappie	65°
Most sunfish	65°
Chain pickerel	63°
Muskellunge	63°
Northern pike	63°
Smallmouth bass	62°
Walleye	58°
Coho salmon	54°
Brook trout	50°
Brown trout	50°
Smelt	50°
Rainbow trout	47°

5. Camouflage and Coloration

Saltwater fish, those that live in the vast oceans of the world, are well known for their many ways of hiding and camouflaging themselves. Freshwater fish, too, exhibit an interesting array of ways to avoid being detected by man, predators, and other fish.

COUNTERSHADING

Did you ever notice how most animals are dark above and light below? As a bird is viewed from below, its light belly does

This muskellunge exhibits countershading—dark above and light below.

not contrast greatly with the bright sky. A hawk looking down on a place where a rabbit is hiding will not be able to see it plainly because the dark back blends with the earth's dark floor.

This form of camouflage is known as *countershading*.

Most fish are countershaded because in their watery environment they experience the same problems of hiding and hunting as do the land animals.

DISRUPTIVE COLORATION

Many species of fish, especially the larger ones, are dressed in patterns of bars, stripes, bands, spots, and swirls. This *disruptive coloration* serves to camouflage a fish in its watery home.

A yellow perch is decorated with heavy, dark bars on its sides to break up the body outline. The muskellunge has a dark

The rainbow trout's disruptive spots, right, break up its outline against the rocky stream bottom.

These yellow perch, below, have dark bars which camouflage them in the weeds among which they swim. Here, on the ice, the bars show up well.

back and light belly and its sides have a series of bars. These irregular bars camouflage the musky as it swims among the grasses looking for other fish. These vertical markings are suggestive of the shadows made by sunlight filtering through the weed beds.

Trout live in fast-flowing streams with stony bottoms. Their spotted bellies and dark backs serve to break up their body outlines and help to conceal them among the many small stones on the stream floor. The tiny sculpin is a master of camouflage. Its mottled color patterns make it practically invisible to both predators and humans.

As the term disruptive coloration suggests, the various color patterns of fish do not make them invisible to an observer. Instead they disrupt the fishes' body outlines so that they are harder to detect.

CHANGING COLORS AND PATTERNS
Like chameleons, some fish are "quick-change artists" when the need arises. These color changes come about slowly by a

The pumpkinseed can change its pattern and colors in seconds.

This baby rainbow trout will change its color and pattern as it gets older and moves to a different habitat.

chemical change in the bloodstream or through a faster method whereby a fish's brain activates special pigment cells in the skin.

Bass have the ability to change their hues to darker over a dark bottom and lighter over a light bottom. The yellow perch can quickly fade from a bright to pale yellow.

Over a longer period of time, fingerlings of many species of fish gradually change their patterns and colors. As they grow and move into new habitats, largemouth bass fingerlings lose their yellowish-brown color and vertical body stripes. Young trout possess dark side patches which they gradually lose as they grow to adults.

BLENDING

Some fish blend with their environment because of special markings, while others are camouflaged because they have no disruptive colors at all.

Bottom-dwelling fishes, such as catfish, sturgeon, eels, scul-

40

The back of this American eel blends well with the stream and river floors on which it feeds and hides.

pins, suckers, and carp, possess few markings of any kind. Instead their colors are uniformly black, brown, or greenish-brown to match them to a drab river or lake bottom. Some of them even burrow into the bottom mud or gravel so that only their eyes, nose, and mouth are sticking out.

CONSPICUOUS COLORATION

Some fish seem to completely reverse the principle of camouflage by advertising their presence. The American shad, for example, is lightly olive-colored over the back and silvery across the rest of its body. These bright, reflective colors enable shad to identify one another and stay together in schools. Most species of minnows also exhibit silvery colors so that they can identify one another as well as stay together in large schools.

Some fish biologists feel that the silvery sides of a fish actually reflect its surroundings like a mirror. Since the fish's body takes on the exact shade of the water, it is difficult to detect the fish's body outline.

The male brook trout is brightly colored at spawning time.

A few of our most beautifully colored fish seem to disregard camouflage at spawning time. The male brook trout, pumpkinseed, redbelly dace, rainbow darter, and kokanee salmon all take on bright breeding colors at the peaks of their spawning periods.

At this time the need for recognition and attraction of a mate tends to become more important than the need for camouflage.

42

6. Predators, Parasites, and Pollution

Throughout their entire lives fish must be ever-alert for the predators that seek to feed on them. Whether finned or furred, feathered or human, chances are that only a very small percentage of the eggs laid by a spawning fish will ever become adults.

Even those that do avoid the jaws of hungry predators may find themselves parasitized by some other living thing. And, possibly worst of all, man's myriad forms of pollution may spell instant death for thousands of fish in a lake, stream, or river. In other places pollution makes it impossible for any fish to exist and the water may be completely void of any life at all.

PREDATORS ABOVE AND BELOW

Practically every fish that swims can, itself, be considered a predator. Naturally, the smaller fishes, such as minnows and darters, feed on microscopic plant and animal matter throughout their lifetimes. The fry of most game fish also feed on these same foods but soon graduate to crayfish, insects and their larvae, tadpoles, frogs, and other fish.

Because the eggs of almost all of the freshwater fish develop outside the females' bodies, other fish, turtles, tadpoles, and salamanders may eat them. Once the eggs hatch and the young

The common water snake, left, is a predator on sickly and slow-moving fish. The American egret, right, like most herons, feeds on fish.

are on their own, they become fair game for herons, turtles, snakes, and, most importantly, other predatory fish. Even some parents, such as trout, are not averse to eating young of their own kind.

As a fish grows, its chances of becoming a meal for a predator decrease. But even the largest can be caught by hook and line and fishermen pride themselves on catching the longest and heaviest.

PARASITES INSIDE AND OUT

Like practically every other wild creature, fish play host to a great many parasites. These may be external (outside) parasites such as leeches and lamprey eels (see Chapter 11) or internal ones like flatworms or tapeworms.

One of the most unusual parasitic relationships involving fish is that of the freshwater mussel (clam) larvae.

The tiny mussel larvae clamp onto the gills and fins of the fish and travel about on them until they mature and drop off. The fish is never harmed by this particular type of parasite.

This fish, above, is infected with a parasite known as anchor worm.

The leech, right, is a common external parasite of fish and other water animals.

POLLUTION

Two types of pollution affect fresh waters and the fish and other life forms that live there.

Inorganic pollution—the type that results from factory wastes, chemicals, mine acids, oils, household detergents, and various other sources—sometimes renders a lake, stream, or river completely unfit for any living things.

These sunfish suffocated in their watery home from organic pollutants.

The most common pollutants are *organic* in nature. These may be in a variety of forms such as sewage or cannery and paper mill wastes.

A small amount of organic pollution may increase the fertility of a body of water. This means that the plants growing in the water will use the organic materials as they decompose.

If there is too much organic material, however, a large amount of the water's oxygen will be used and undesirable gases may be produced. The fish in these waters then suffocate.

A third form of pollution—known as *thermal* pollution—involves no foreign materials at all. Factories and powerplants often use vast quantities of water for cooling purposes. Even though the water had nothing added or taken away, it is simply too warm for the stream or river life and death is the result.

Some fish—such as trout—are very sensitive to oxygen-using and temperature-changing pollution, while others, such as carp and garfish, are quite tolerant.

7. Ancient Freshwater Fish

The sturgeon, paddlefish, gar, and bowfin might well be called "living fossils." They existed back when dinosaurs roamed the land, and still swim in some of our fresh waters today.

STURGEONS

Seven different species of sturgeons dwell in North America's waters. All live in fresh water at least part of their lifetimes. The white and green sturgeons ascend the rivers of the Pacific Coast at spawning time, and the Atlantic and shortnose sturgeons do the same in the East. The lake, shovelnose, and pallid sturgeons are exclusively freshwater fishes.

The sturgeons resemble, in practically every way, the prehistoric creatures, which they really are. They have very few body scales and possess five (sometimes seven) lengthwise rows of bony humps—one row along the back and two others along the middle and bottom on each side. On young sturgeons these humps may be tipped with a tapered ridge and a spine. As the fish grow older, however, the humps become blunted and may disappear entirely.

Sturgeons are known to live 50 to 150 years. Three of them— the lake, white, and Atlantic sturgeons—have the distinction of

The Atlantic sturgeon grows to about 6 feet and 350 pounds.

being our largest freshwater fishes. In October of 1897, an 1800-pound white sturgeon was taken at Mission, British Columbia. The Atlantic sturgeon seldom grows larger than 350 pounds and the lake sturgeon slightly less.

In the spring or early summer, saltwater-dwelling sturgeons move up North America's larger rivers to spawn. A large female might shed as many as 4 million eggs, which she "broadcasts" over the river floor. In a week or so small sturgeon larvae hatch. They live in the river for one to three years before migrating to the sea. Sturgeons that live their entire lives in fresh water seek swift-flowing tributaries or clean, lake-bottom gravel at spawning time.

Even though female sturgeons may lay from 2 to 5 million eggs, their survival rate is extremely low. In years past they were thought to be "pest fish," and when captured in the nets of commercial fishermen were tossed along the banks to rot or to be carted off as food for hogs. In the mid-1800s, though, the sturgeon became known for its tasty flesh and the value of its roe (eggs) for caviar. In 1890, 5 million pounds of sturgeon were taken from the Delaware River alone. Today the results of overfishing, industrial pollutants, and the building of dams

48

which blocked the migration to their spawning places have combined to greatly reduce the populations of all sturgeons.

WHITE STURGEON—*Acipenser transmontanus*

Known variously as the Pacific Coast sturgeon, Oregon sturgeon, Sacramento sturgeon, and Columbia River sturgeon, this species reportedly attains a weight of 1,800 pounds, though 300 to 400 pounds tends to be average. Due to its large size and long life (some are believed to live for 150 years), the white sturgeon does not reach maturity until it is about 15 years old.

GREEN STURGEON—*Acipenser medirostris*

The green sturgeon is the other Pacific Coast member of the family. Unlike the white sturgeon, this species is more frequently found in salt or brackish water. In size it averages under 100 pounds, though the maximum record is 350 pounds.

The green sturgeon dwells in the same places as the white, though its populations are concentrated between San Francisco and Puget Sound.

ATLANTIC STURGEON—*Acipenser oxyrhynchus*

Early colonists in New England, Pennsylvania, and New Jersey were impressed by the abundance of giant Atlantic sturgeon in the lower Delaware River. One verified record exists of a 14-footer taken near New Brunswick, Canada, and early settlers boasted of catching 18-foot-long fish. Today it is unusual to find a 6-foot Atlantic sturgeon.

This giant fish browses along the Atlantic Coast throughout the year, feeding on worms and mollusks located by its barbels. In spring, both males and females seek the fresh waters of a tributary river to spawn. As soon as the reproductive process is over, the adults once again return to the sea. The fry stay in fresh water for a year before moving downstream to the ocean.

The Atlantic sturgeon's range stretches from the Gulf of St. Lawrence to the Carolinas.

The shortnose sturgeon is an endangered species in the United States.

Shortnose sturgeon—*Acipenser brevirostrum*

The rare shortnose sturgeon occupies a range similar to that of the Atlantic sturgeon, though it is only present as far north as Cape Cod. To the south, where it is slightly more common, it can be found as far as Florida.

This fish averages only 2 to 3 feet in size. Very little is known of its spawning habits, though it is thought to duplicate that of the larger Atlantic sturgeon.

Lake sturgeon—*Acipenser fulvescens*

This species is strictly a freshwater sturgeon. Records show that it may attain sizes of 8 feet and 300 pounds, though most rarely grow larger than 100 pounds.

Young lake sturgeons possess a strange suction disc on the snout which is used for clinging to stones or vegetation. As they grow to adulthood, the sturgeons lose this disc.

The oldest lake sturgeon ever recorded was a 152-year-old fish.

About 100 years ago, the lake sturgeon industry thrived at several places on the Great Lakes. Besides utilizing the roe and flesh as food, leather was manufactured from sturgeon skins. A few sturgeon fisheries still exist in Canada, though they are nowhere as great as they once were.

SHOVELNOSE STURGEON—*Scaphirhynchus platorynchus*

This sturgeon is quite small, averaging only 4 or 5 pounds.

It is found in the Mississippi-Missouri river systems of the United States. Because of its size it has never been considered commercially important.

The shovelnose sturgeon is small compared to others of its family.

PALLID STURGEON —*Scaphirhynchus albus*

This sturgeon is somewhat larger than the shovelnose and inhabits a similar range. It may grow to 15 pounds and 4 feet in length.

Called the rock sturgeon in some areas, it is bluish-gray in comparison to the yellow-brown coloration of the shovelnose.

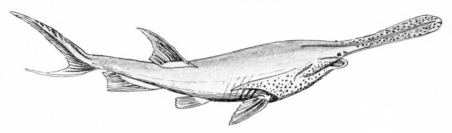

The paddlefish is one of America's strangest looking fish.

Paddlefish

Paddlefish—*Polyodon spathula*

There's no stranger-looking creature than the paddlefish. Though a distant relative of the sturgeons, it is not as common and only inhabits scattered deep rivers and lakes in the United States.

The fish's name comes from its snout which extends into a broad flattened paddlelike organ about half as long as the fish's body. As it swims, the mouth is kept open so that the current carries plankton, its main food, into it.

The paddlefish can grow to 150 pounds, though 60 to 90 pounders are average today.

Past overfishing, dams, and pollution have reduced the paddlefish's populations to very low numbers throughout its range.

Gars

The entire gar family, of which there are five species, possess a characteristic cylindrical body and an elongated, heavily toothed mouth. They are warm-water fish occurring in lakes, bayous, and slow-moving rivers of the southern states and Mexico. Two species can be found in the Great Lakes.

The food of gars is entirely fish, with the exception of the alligator gar which eats anything from worms to reptiles and birds.

They spawn in the spring, and the mating operation simply

52

involves the broadcasting of eggs and sperm over the vegetation in a weedy shallow. The unconcerned parents neither build a nest nor guard the eggs or young.

The gar's scales are armorlike, diagonally arranged, and so tough that they were once used by Indians as arrow tips.

Gars have a habit of resting at the surface, breathing air, and suddenly lunging at their prey with great speed. They will slash at prey with their needlelike teeth until the panicked fish is finally caught.

ALLIGATOR GAR—*Lepisosteus spatula*

This is the largest of the five gars. Legends of the Deep South tell of alligator gars 15 to 20 feet long, though such fish have never actually been authenticated. Specimens 5 to 6 feet in length are common and others to slightly under 10 feet have been recorded.

This fish lives in the sluggish waters of the southern states and northern Mexico.

It is so named because of its size and the alligatorlike appearance of its head.

LONGNOSE GAR—*Lepisosteus osseus*

The longnose gar averages 3 to 4 feet in size. It lives in the lower Great Lakes, down through the Mississippi basin and the Gulf Coast.

A pair of longnose gars

The spotted gar is named for the many spots across its body.

The shortnose gar, below, closely resembles the long-nose gar but with a slightly shorter beak and fewer spots.

SPOTTED GAR—*Lepisosteus ocalatus*

The spotted gar is rather small, averaging about 8 feet in length. It is named for the large dark spots on the dorsal, anal, and caudal fins and the top of the head.

It occurs in Lake Erie and southward in the Mississippi and Missouri rivers.

SHORTNOSE GAR—*Lepisosteus platostomus*

Despite its name, this fish closely resembles the longnose gar except for the obvious difference—the shorter nose. The spots are also not as common across the body and fins.

The shortnose rarely grows longer than 3 feet. It lives in the southern Mississippi-Missouri system of water.

FLORIDA GAR—*Lepisosteus platyrhincus*

The Florida gar is about the same size as the shortnose species and lives in a small area of coastal streams in Florida and Georgia.

The Florida gar lives in a small area of coastal streams in Florida and Georgia.

BOWFIN

BOWFIN—*Amia calva*

The bowfin's main identifying feature is its long, spineless dorsal fin, which extends along the back to the base of the tail. It is a relatively small fish compared to the sturgeons and gars, averaging only 3 or 5 pounds.

The bowfin's long dorsal fin is a good identifying feature.

Like many other of the ancient fishes, the bowfin has an air bladder which is used to breathe air at the surface.

Known also as a "dogfish," the bowfin's range is limited to the sluggish waters of the Mississippi basin and eastward to the Great Lakes and Vermont.

This fish is strictly carnivorous, and scientists have discovered that its diet may be composed of almost 60 percent game fish.

At spawning time the male bowfin builds a round nest in which several females may lay their eggs. They are then fertilized and guarded through hatching and until the young are able to fend for themselves.

The adult bowfin averages about 3 or 5 pounds.

8. Game Fish

Any of our larger fishes that are sporty enough to put up a battle on the end of a line are known as "game fish." They vary greatly in size from the smaller stocked trout to 30- and 40-pound muskellunge.

MUSKELLUNGE—*Esox masquinongy*
The musky occurs in Canada and the northeastern United States and is the largest of the common game fish. Its great size and fighting qualities make it one of the most prized fish that can be caught on rod and reel.

The three pike family members are sometimes difficult to distinguish.

The true muskellunge is our largest freshwater game fish. Some large specimens exceed 65 pounds and 5½ feet.

The musky prefers medium-sized lakes and large rivers where it lies in wait for unsuspecting fish. With a sudden burst of speed, it swims forward and grabs its prey crosswise between tooth-studded jaws. On occasion it will also take ducklings, small muskrats, and even its own young.

At spawning time, in April or May, lake muskies seek shallow, weed-infested bays to lay their eggs. The fry grow to 8 inches their first year of life and by the time they are four years of age may have attained a length of 2½ feet.

NORTHERN PIKE—*Esox lucius*

Anglers often call the northern pike the "lone wolf" of fresh water. Tales of "devil lakes" in the Yukon are told by Eskimos

The northern pike is often called the lone wolf because of its feeding habits.

who believe that monster pike capable of swallowing man and canoe dwell there.

Though the pike certainly does not grow to such size, it averages 2 to 10 pounds and often much larger in Canada. What it may lack in size comparison to its cousin, the musky, it makes up in sheer savagery.

It hunts by waiting patiently in the weedy shallows. When a smaller fish moves near, the pike lurches forward and grabs it crosswise in its jaws. It then swims off a short distance to devour its prize.

In the spring a female pike, usually accompanied by one or more smaller males, moves near some shallow shore. Here she broadcasts up to 250,000 adhesive eggs (from a 30-pound fish) which stick to whatever they touch. In about two weeks, the eggs hatch into fry which almost immediately begin their predatory lives.

The small lone wolves first feed on microscopic life, then graduate to insects, worms, minnows, and even smaller young of their own kind.

CHAIN PICKEREL—*Esox niger*

To see a chain pickerel is to understand where it gets its name. A pattern of black chainlike markings runs along each

The chain pickerel gets its name from a pattern of chainlike markings on its sides.

side from cheek to tail. At first appearance they resemble a series of chains against the pickerel's greenish body.

The chain pickerel does not grow nearly as large as its cousins —the pike and the musky. Like these two fishes, however, it lays its eggs in weedy shallows of lakes and rivers. It is one of the earliest fish to spawn, often laying its eggs before the winter ice is completely gone.

As a game fish the pickerel is popular, though even an 18-incher contains relatively little meat. Though it averages 15 to 20 inches in length, a pickerel rarely exceeds 3 pounds.

The record chain pickerel taken by rod and reel, in Georgia, was a relative "giant" weighing 9½ pounds and measuring 31 inches.

BROOK TROUT—*Salvelinus fontinalis*

Strange as it may seem to most anglers, this beautiful fish is actually a "char" and not a "trout." There really isn't all that much difference to the anglers, though scientists place it in the char group because of the presence of a toothed bone in the center of the mouth. Since this feature differs in fishes grouped as chars and trout, the brook trout is a char.

The brook trout is often called the native or brookie in the northeastern United States and Canada.

This is the "native trout" of the northeastern United States and Canada. It is often found in small streams, but it also frequents cold-water lakes, ponds, and rivers. In Canada it is usually called "speckled trout."

The brook trout is easily distinguished from its cousins by brilliant red spots with blue rims on its sides, a brownish-green back with dark wavy lines, lower fins edged in white, and a "square" tail. In fall, when they spawn, the male "brookies'" bellies turn an orangish-red.

The brook trout's normal food includes a variety of stream insects, minnows, freshwater shrimp, crayfish, and land insects, such as grasshoppers that fall into the stream. One of its favorite foods—the caddisworm—lives in a stone "house" which the brook trout has learned to find. Quite often an angler will find stones in a brook trout's stomach as it is being prepared for the frying pan.

In the northeastern part of the country millions of brook trout are raised in hatcheries and put into streams prior to the trout season. But in some places, where cold mountain waters run clear and clean, the native variety still reproduces just as it did years back before man's pollution reduced its numbers.

This 33-pound, 10-ounce, brown trout was caught in Utah's Flaming Gorge Reservoir on March 4, 1977, by Robert Bringhurst. The 48-inch fish broke the existing world's record by 2 pounds.

BROWN TROUT—*Salmo trutta*

The brown trout came to the United States from Germany almost a hundred years ago (in 1882) in the form of fertile eggs. These eggs hatched into fry, grew into adults, and in turn produced more eggs. The process still continues today— the results of those first eggs brought over on an ocean liner. Later other brown trout were imported from Germany, England, and Scotland.

The "brownie" can tolerate temperatures about 5 degrees warmer than a brook trout. Though the difference seems very slight, it enables the brown trout to live in waters, such as large rivers, that the brook trout cannot tolerate.

The color of the brownie is not always brown. Sometimes it is more of a bronze-green with golden yellow undersides. Regardless of the base color, this fish is always decorated with large black or brown spots intermixed with some red spots.

Like the brook trout, the brown trout spawns in autumn. They will usually enter a tributary or small stream to mate. Here the female scoops out three or four nests in which she deposits up to 6,000 large, nonadhesive eggs.

The brownie lives longer and grows larger than the brookie. Several American brown trout have been caught that weighed in excess of 20 pounds, though half that size is a good trophy.

Rainbow trout—*Salmo gairdneri*

On the West Coast, the rainbow trout enters salt water for part of its life and is known as the "steelhead." Throughout the rest of its present range, the rainbow lives its entire life in fresh water.

This colorful fish's original range was confined to the fast-flowing rivers of the Pacific Coast from California to Alaska. Plantings have now established it throughout the northern part of the United States and into Canada.

The name "rainbow" is actually a misleading one, for the main color shown by this trout is a pinkish-lavender. All over its body it has many small dark spots.

Unlike the brook and brown trouts, the rainbow is a spring

Plantings have now established the rainbow trout throughout the northern portions of North America.

spawner. It seeks a place where there is plenty of oxygen and little chance that the eggs will be covered by silt in the streams. The tail end of a deep pool usually suits it just fine.

Anglers often argue over which of the familiar trout provides the greatest challenge, though most agree that the rainbow is the best fighter. When hooked it will battle both under and atop the water, often leaping like a salmon in hopes of ridding itself of the hook and line.

Lake trout—*Salvelinus namaycush*

Even though many kinds of trout live in lakes, this species is the only one properly called "lake" trout.

Like its cousin, the brook trout, the lake trout is really a member of the char family.

Over much of the range in which it can be found, it is called the "laker." This range covers much of the width of Canada

Well-known outdoor writer Ben Callaway hoists three Quebec lake trout.

and Alaska, as well as the United States from the Great Lakes eastward.

One of the requirements of the beautiful laker is deep water. When the hot months of July and August warm surface waters, *namaycush* dives deep and stays there until the cool autumn breezes once more cool the top waters.

In the fall, the lake trout chooses the opposite extreme to spawn in about 15 feet of water over some rocky bottom. Some, however, like the lake trout that inhabit the Great Lakes, spawn over clay bottoms in much deeper waters.

Depending on water temperature, the eggs hatch out in anywhere from seven to twenty-three weeks—the warmer the water, the faster their development. The young trout are believed to seek deep waters upon hatching, here feeding on shrimp, other crustaceans, insects, and worms. As the fish grow, their diets become entirely piscivorous (fish-eating) and larger fish are eaten.

The color of the laker ranges from gray through brown to green, depending on where it lives. Its belly is white and occasionally slightly pink. It has black spots across the full length of its body.

WALLEYE—*Stizostedion vitreum*

If any fish can be described as "ghostlike," it is surely the walleye. Its large cloudy-looking eyes give it the appearance of being blind.

Unlike the trouts, the walleye is considered a warm-water fish even though it thrives across northern Canada in frigid waters where the basses can't live. It is common in the Great Lakes and throughout the major river systems of northern America.

The walleye's color is basically dark greenish-brown with brassy sides. Its belly is white.

The fact that the walleye's general body shape resembles

that of the yellow perch is no coincidence. The perch, along with the walleye—and even the small Johnny darter—make up the family Percidae. It also has a look-alike but lesser-known relative called the sauger.

Just because the perch is a relative makes no difference to the walleye when hungry. Perch, sunfish, and minnows, as well as the fry of other game fish, make up the major portion of the walleye's diet.

The walleye is an impatient spawner, often beginning its spring reproduction activities before the break-up of winter's ice. Depending upon where they live, the choice of egg-laying sites may be along a rocky shoreline or upstream in some swift-flowing tributary.

To the serious fisherman the walleye is a challenge to hook and line and a treat on the table. Its flaky white meat is second to none among those who like fish.

The author battles a walleye on Pennsylvania's Pine Creek.

The largemouth bass is probably the most popular game fish in the country.

LARGEMOUTH BASS—*Micropterus salmoides*

It can safely be said that more money is spent on the large-mouth bass than any other species of North American fish. In recent years bass fishing clubs, and even professional bass fishermen, have come on the scene. Millions of dollars are spent annually on boats, baits, rods, reels, and travel to fish for *Micropterus salmoides*.

The largemouth's scientific name means "salmonlike or trout-like, with a small fin"—a name hardly descriptive of this fish. None of this fish's fins can be considered "small," nor is it "troutlike" in shape. Instead the dorsal fin is long and the body chunky and deep.

Strange as it may seem, the basses—both the largemouth and the smallmouth—belong to the sunfish family. Not surprisingly, they're the family's largest members.

Largemouth bass grow larger in the South where they have

67

Charles Heidecker lifts a "lunker" largemouth from a Pocono Mountain, Pennsylvania, lake. Note the artificial rubber frog hanging from the fish's mouth.

a longer growing season. That is, the lakes there do not freeze, and heavy feeding takes place year around.

Largemouth bass spawn in shallow waters in late spring. At this time they seek a mud-bottomed shoreline where a crude nest is scraped in the vegetation. The male bass entices a female to lay her eggs in the nest, which he immediately fertilizes. From that time on the female is no longer concerned about the eggs—except for a possible return trip to the nest to shed a few more. Or else she may find the nest of a different male to lay her late-ripening eggs.

The male largemouth is an excellent guardian. From the time the eggs are laid until they hatch, he keeps a wary eye for intruders. All the while he's on sentinel duty he fans the eggs to keep them well oxygenated and free of silt, fungus, and small predators. He will even stay with the brood until the yolk sac is used up. After that, the fry scatter and his nesting chores are finished.

Adult bass feed on a 60 percent fish diet. The rest of their foods include worms, leeches, crayfish, frogs, and practically anything else small enough to swallow—including any mice that happen to splash around the edge of a pond or lake.

Fishermen refer to big bass as "lunkers" or, in the South, "hawgs" (hogs). Small overpopulated ponds, however, will contain few large bass and plenty of small, stunted ones.

SMALLMOUTH BASS—*Micropterus dolomieui*

The smallmouth and the largemouth basses are similar in appearance, though there are several identifying marks to distinguish one from the other.

Most largemouths possess a dark horizontal bar along each side and are dark green in color. Smallmouths are bronze with several dark vertical bars on their sides.

The smallmouth's mouth is actually not all that "small" except by comparison to the largemouth's.

Another feature that fishermen use to determine whether the fish they catch is a largemouth or smallmouth is the structure of the dorsal fin. In a largemouth, this fin is so deeply notched in the middle that it appears as two fins. The smallmouth has

The smallmouth prefers colder water than its largemouth cousin.

69

the front and back parts of the dorsal more broadly joined.

The smallmouth originally lived in the Great Lakes drainage but now can be found wherever the clean, cool waters of rocky lakes and rivers provide it a home. It is more of a cold-water enthusiast than its big-mouthed cousin.

The smallmouth's spawning habits are much the same as the largemouth's. If anything, the male smallmouth builds a much neater nest, often lined with sand and gravel around the edges circling larger stones.

White bass—*Roccus chrysops*

This is a member of the family known as "true basses." Its best-known relative is the striped bass, which migrates up river tributaries from its ocean home.

Some people believe that the white bass is actually the result of striped bass that became landlocked many years ago. Scientists, however, do not go along with this theory. The six to eight dark narrow stripes running along the white bass's silvery body serve to identify it.

Like many other species of fish, this bass has been stocked in other waters, though its native range is that surrounding the Great Lakes and its drainage systems.

Even though the young bass grow rapidly, they do not get very large. Most of those caught by hook and line weigh only about a pound. The world's record caught in Mississippi, however, scaled out at slightly over 5 pounds.

The female white bass makes no nest but instead scatters her eggs with little concern for them. This method leaves the eggs open to much predation, but the fact that a large fish lays about a half-million eggs more than makes up for the losses.

The fry feed on small insects and crustaceans, and graduate to small fish as they grow. In some lakes the white bass thrives on microscopic *Daphnia*.

70

An Arctic grayling

ARCTIC GRAYLING—*Thymallus arcticus*

The arctic grayling is not known to the average angler. It lives in the north country—far beyond the cities and towns of man— all across the top of Canada into Alaska and as far north as the Arctic Ocean.

At one time the grayling lived in Michigan and Montana but, surprisingly, no state in between. It is believed to have become extinct in Michigan in 1930—mainly because logging of its streambanks caused warming of the cool waters it needed to live and spawn.

The grayling's most distinctive feature is its large dorsal fin, which resembles that of a small sailfish. When hooked or excited at spawning time, the fin is held erect and the fish appears much larger than its average foot-long size.

The grayling is bluish in coloration with a dozen or more black spots on the front sides.

One unusual feature of this fish, reported by a number of anglers and writers, is that it smells like thyme. Thyme is an herb with a lemony odor that can be found on the spice shelves of many homes.

The grayling's main food is insects—of practically all aquatic and terrestrial varieties. For this reason fly fishermen consider the grayling a true challenge and take distant trips to its cold-water home for the sake of catching it on an artificial fly.

71

9. Panfish and Catfish

Some of the most familiar freshwater fishes are "panfish" and "catfish." As the name implies, "panfish" are fishes typically small enough to place whole in a frying pan. Catfish have fleshy "whiskers" which aid them in finding food and have the appearance of cat's whiskers.

Farm ponds and city reservoirs across the country frequently have populations of both panfish and catfish. The bluegill, pumpkinseed, or bullhead is often the first catch of a boy or girl's angling career.

The "sunfish family," which includes such relatives as the bluegill, pumpkinseed, crappie bass, rock bass, and a variety of others, is well represented in the panfish category. All members of this family spawn in the spring or early summer and are chiefly carnivorous.

The catfish clan numbers 24 different species in North America. They range in size from the small "stonecats" and "madtoms"—averaging only about 4 inches in length—to the monstrous blue catfish which is known sometimes to reach 150 pounds. Members of the catfish family are tough and rugged, surviving temperatures and degrees of pollution that would kill other more-sensitive fish.

The sunfish family includes the crappie bass, bluegill, and pumpkinseed shown here. It also includes the largemouth and smallmouth basses, though they are too big to be considered as panfish.

Like bats and owls on land, catfish are largely night creatures. They prowl about the floors of their watery homes in search of practically anything edible, including small fish, fish eggs, worms, plants, and even fruits and seeds that drop in from above.

None of the catfish have scales, and all species possess eight barbels which are sensitive to taste and touch. Three stiff spines, one at the front of the dorsal fin and one at each of the two pectoral fins, protect the catfish from predators.

It was recently learned that each of these spines holds a mild poison secreted by the skin. The poison may sting should a spine break the skin of a person's hand, but it is not considered dangerous.

73

The bluegill is the sunfish with the greatest range.

BLUEGILL—*Lepomis macrochirus*

This is most likely the "sunfish" with the greatest range. In the northern states it's the bluegill, but southerners call it "bream" (pronounced "brim"), or copperhead.

The bluegill is a colorful creature, especially at mating time when the breast turns a bright shade of reddish-orange. Young bluegills usually have striped sides, but as they get older these stripes disappear and the blue-green color is predominant.

The bluegill can be distinguished from its relatives by dark blue gill flaps—sometimes referred to as "ears."

A bluegill's "average" size is hard to pinpoint. Where it is overcrowded the fish may only be 4 or 5 inches in length, while other lakes and ponds can have specimens of 9 to 12 inches.

At spawning time the male fans out a nest in shallow water. Often dozens of these nests can be detected along a shoreline. A female deposits her eggs in the nest—as many as 50,000 from a

74

large female—and leaves the duties of motherhood to the male.

Few farm ponds across the country are without bluegills and largemouth bass which feed on them and keep them in balance. Both of these fishes can stand warm temperatures—a necessity of fish living in shallow ponds and lakes.

PUMPKINSEED—*Lepomis gibbosus*

This is the common "sunny" of every adult's childhood memories. Though many fish prefer shady locations, the pumpkinseed is a sun-worshiper and can frequently be seen out in the open in places that other fish thoroughly avoid.

The pumpkinseed is truly one of the most beautiful of all freshwater fish. Besides an array of colors ranging from a purplish-blue through red, green, and yellow, the primary identifying mark is a small red spot on each ear flap.

Though its mouth is quite small, the sunny has strong teeth in its throat to break the mollusks and crustaceans it regularly eats.

The colorful pumpkinseed is often referred to simply as the sunny.

This exceptionally large black crappie, left, was caught in Pennsylvania's Lake Wallenpaupack. Right, an ice fisherman removes a white crappie from the hook.

The black crappie bass

The pumpkinseed may spawn several times throughout the summer in a manner similar to that of the bluegill. In fact, pumpkinseeds and bluegills often interbreed to produce hybrids resembling both parents in certain facets.

BLACK CRAPPIE—*Pomoxis nigromaculatus*
WHITE CRAPPIE—*Pomoxis annularis*

Not considering the smallmouth and largemouth basses, the two species of crappie bass are the largest members of the sunfish family.

Both species resemble one another, though the black crappie tends to be darker, as its name implies. The white crappie is more silver in coloration and lacks the dark vertical bars of its cousin.

Throughout their ranges (the black is more common in the North, the white down South) these two fishes have no less than 55 common names. "Calico bass," "strawberry bass," "bachelor," "white bass," and "papermouth" are just a few of them.

The latter name—papermouth—comes from the crappie's soft mouth which sometimes tears from the hook.

The crappies spawn as early as January in Florida to early July in the northernmost states. Just after spawning they seem to go on a feeding spree and anglers have their best success.

ROCK BASS—*Amblopites rupestris*

Unlike the other members of the sunfish family, the rock bass is not a very colorful character. Its greenish-brown back lightens to a brassy color on the sides and a pale gray belly. Its one outstanding feature is its red eyes—accounting for its nicknames of "redeye" and "goggle-eye." A dark blue-black dot at the tip of each gill cover is another reliable identifying mark.

The rock bass prefers a habitat similar to that of the smallmouth bass. Clear-flowing water with an abundance of rocks

The rock bass is often called the "goggle-eye" because of its large red eyes.

and cold lakes with deep holes are suitable homes for this scrappy little fish.

Anglers seldom fish specifically for rock bass but often catch them when trying for smallmouth bass. Since the goggle-eye has the largest mouth of all the smaller sunfishes, it will often strike plugs almost as large as itself.

The rock bass's spawning habits are similar to that of other sunfish—single nests in the gravel or sand near some protection.

The average size of this fish is about 8 inches, though some do grow larger.

Another fish, the warmouth, very closely resembles the rock bass. Though present at various places in the Northeast, it is much more common to the South and West.

YELLOW PERCH—*Perca flavescens*

The yellow perch is considered a pest or a prize, depending on its size and whether he's caught on purpose or not. In some ponds and lakes it has a tendency to overpopulate and stunted fish are the only ones available.

The perch, and its close relative, the walleye, differ from the sunfish by having two distinct and separate dorsal fins—the front one with strong spines and the rear soft-rayed.

The basic color pattern of the yellow perch is a greenish-yellow body, with six to eight dark vertical bands on each side. A white belly and brilliant orange fins, at spawning time, complete its natural dress.

Just after the ice on a lake breaks up, the perch begin their spawning. The females shed their eggs haphazardly in long, gelatinous strings. After the eggs are fertilized, the jellylike covering of the eggs swells considerably.

It takes eight to ten days for the eggs to hatch, at which time the young are immediately on their own.

In the balance of nature of a pond or lake, the perch is important as food for larger game fishes such as bass, walleye, pike, and muskies.

As tablefare the yellow perch is second to none. Ice fishermen frequently take portable camp stoves out on the ice with them and fry the flaky, white meat of their fresh catches soon after pulling them through the holes.

The yellow perch is a member of the same scientific family as the walleye.

The author's son, Andy, with a brown bullhead caught in the Delaware River

BROWN BULLHEAD—*Ictalurus nebulosus*
YELLOW BULLHEAD—*Ictalurus natalis*
BLACK BULLHEAD—*Ictalurus melas*

The total range of these three species of bullhead catfish covers practically the entire United States and southern Canada.

The brown bullhead, ofttimes called the "horned pout" in the North, is the most common of the three similar species. It thrives in a variety of habitats, including warm lakes and cold creeks.

80

The yellow bullhead is readily identified by its lighter amber coloration. It is primarily a dweller of ponds and lakes in both the North and South.

The black bullhead is a rarity in the Far North but is quite common in the Midwest. It, like the yellow, likes the warmth of lakes and ponds.

All of the bullheads are generally small—averaging 9 to 12 inches in length, though they do grow larger.

Both the males and females have the unusual habit of inhaling their jellylike egg clusters and then spitting them out again. Biologists believe that this is done to rid the eggs of siltation and provide them with oxygen.

As the fry hatch, they gather enmasse and swim about for a few days under the guard of one or both of their parents.

The bullheads are catfish that double as panfish since their biological make-up and small size qualifiy them as both.

Despite their small size, bullheads are rugged fishes. They can even survive out of the water for an amazingly long time.

Here is a close-up look at the mouth and whiskers of a black bullhead catfish.

The channel catfish has dark spots on its sides and a deeply forked tail.

CHANNEL CATFISH—*Ictalurus punctatus*

The "channel cat" could readily qualify as a game fish, for many anglers seek it for its sporting qualities and for food.

The channel catfish's typical colors are silver-gray through light brown—depending on its environment. Regardless of the base color, its sides are decorated with dark spots of varied sizes.

In some places it is called the "spotted cat" because of these distinctive markings.

Its tail is deeply forked—a good identification feature.

The channel cat's size averages 5 to 20 pounds in some waters and only 4 to 5 in others. The world record, caught in a South Carolina lake, weighed 57 pounds—proving that it can grow much larger than "average."

At spawning time in the spring, the fish seeks the seclusion of overhanging banks or even submerged muskrat holes or hollow logs. The male guards the eggs throughout incubation and even shepherds the youngsters about until they are able to fend for themselves.

BLUE CATFISH—*Ictalurus furcatus*

The blue catfish is the family giant. Though most of them caught by rod and reel range from 15 to 30 pounds, records of "blues" going 100 pounds or more are not unusual. There is one verified record of a 150-pound specimen.

This catfish is blue-gray in coloration with a silvery-white

Blue catfish weighing 100 pounds caught in a Tennessee lake

belly. Its tail is deeply forked and the top jaw visibly protrudes past the bottom one.

The blue cat is a denizen of large, slow-moving rivers from the Midwest and South.

In years past this fish was caught with "brush lines." These were baited lines attached to trees and brushes in areas of the lower Mississippi that flooded each spring.

The catfish would leave their river homes and follow the floodwaters. As they sought food they would be caught by the brush lines, which were checked regularly by the fishermen who placed them.

FLATHEAD CATFISH—*Pylodictus olivarus*

Like the blue cat, the "flathead" prefers large sluggish rivers. Anglers may tie into individuals weighing anywhere from 2 to 50 pounds, and specimens of 100 pounds are known to exist.

In the lower Mississippi River they are netted commercially and, along with other species of catfish, make up a very important food fishery.

The flathead is more of a fish-eater than most of the other catfish. At night it swims into shallow waters to seek food.

Where the flathead catfish gets its name is obvious to anyone

The flathead catfish is identified by its long, flat wide head.

who has seen it. It is both long and flat, made to look as grotesque as any fish by the lower jaw which extends beyond the upper.

Like most other members of the family, the flatheads are good parents. The females first lay eggs at about four years of age and reproduce each spring throughout their 20-year life-span.

Because of a strange liking for submerged, hollow logs in which to hide or spawn, some flatheads never live their full lives. Sometimes one will swim into the log and be unable to get back out—and it becomes its grave.

WHITE CATFISH—*Ictalurus catus*

The white catfish is the smallest of the "big cats." One or 2 pounds is the average weight, though occasionally one is caught weighing four or five times that "average."

Originally it lived only in the eastern and southern United States but it has been stocked in waters as far west as California and north into New England.

Though named "white" catfish, its main color is actually more olive. The belly area, however, is silvery white.

The white catfish is actually greenish-blue to olive on its back and sides and only white (or silvery) below.

10. The Minnow Family

"Minnies" youngsters call them and oldsters usually think of minnows as being *any* small fish. Yet the largest member of this family is known to reach 55 pounds and others may grow anywhere from 1½ to 4 feet long.

A minnow is any member of a group of fishes scientifically called the Cyprinidae. It is estimated that there are about 200 different species of them in North America.

Unlike some freshwater fish that migrate to salt water or live their lives in brackish water, minnows are entirely freshwater inhabitants.

Though there is a great variation in their sizes, all minnows share certain features that account for their classification.

For one, they all have exceptionally large scales across all of the body except the head. Unlike the catfish, whose bodies tend to be flattened from top to bottom, the minnows are compressed from side to side. Most minnows also have a short dorsal fin located in the center of the back.

Another unique feature of the Cyprinidae clan is that their teeth are located in the throat and not in the mouth.

The minnow family has the largest range of any of the continental fish. They are found in the biggest lakes and smallest creeks and have adapted to both warm and cold waters.

At breeding time the males of many of the species take on brilliant hues and develop small horny bumps on their heads.

It takes an expert to identify many of the smaller minnows—a task next to impossible for the average angler.

CARP—*Cyprinus carpio*

The carp is the largest, the oldest, and the best known of all the minnows. Its history dates back to 500 B.C. in China. For hundreds of years it has been used as food in Europe and Asia.

About 150 years ago it was first imported into the United States, though today's populations are the result of importations of only a century ago.

At first the carp was a welcome addition to America, but it slowly wore out its welcome. Wherever it took hold it competed with more desirable species for food and disturbed their spawning waters. To make matters worse the carp also ate the game fish's young and spread new parasites and diseases. Today some midwestern states are undertaking carp control programs to reduce their populations.

Even in normally clear waters the carp can make a mess. It

The carp is the best known of all minnows.

uproots vegetation—disturbing both food and clear water needed for spawning of other fish.

The carp has two pairs of fleshy barbels alongside the mouth. One pair is quite long and readily seen.

Its color is olive-brown on top and somewhat brassy on the sides.

In line with its reckless way of life, the carp sheds its eggs over silty, vegetated shallows and then abandons them. They hatch in one to two weeks.

As they search for food, these oversized minnows have a habit of uprooting aquatic plants. Some of these they eat, along with combinations of insects, mollusks, crustaceans, small fish, fish eggs, and even animal wastes.

Despite their unsavory reputation, carp are still sought by a great number of anglers. They put up a good battle on rod and reel and are still eaten by many people. Several million pounds of carp are eaten in the United States and Canada each year. Most of them are raised by man.

Though not nearly as common, four species of large minnows known as "squawfish" live in the northwestern sector of the country. The best known is the northern or Columbia River squawfish and another, the Colorado squawfish, is considered threatened due to pollution.

The goldfish (*Carassius auratus*) is a look-alike miniature of the carp. Also an import, the goldfish is more of a decorative species than anything else. Those that escape or are released to the wild will lose their bright colors and take on the duller hues of their big cousin.

FALLFISH—*Semotilus corporalis*

The fallfish isn't really considered to be a good fighting fish, though many anglers enjoy catching it. In trout and smallmouth bass waters, the fallfish will strike artificial flies and the same baits used for the other fishes.

A trout fisherman caught these silvery fallfish.

The fallfish gets its name from the simple fact that it is often (but not only) found at the base of waterfalls. Other names for this large, silver minnow include windfish, chub, and corporal.

Corporalis is mainly a northern fish. In spring the male builds an elaborate nest of large mounds of stones inside of which the fertilized eggs mature and hatch.

CREEK CHUB—*Semotilus atromaculatus*

Like the fallfish, the creek chub is also a nest builder of note. Though smaller, its nests are often larger in size (but with smaller stones) than that of the fallfish.

The name "horned dace" is just as common as creek chub in some regions. This name comes from the scattering of small hard "horns" that the male gets on its head and snout at spawning time.

The creek chub is sometimes considered a pest by serious anglers.

This dace prefers to live in clear, flowing water and trout fishermen may consider it a pest at times. It averages 6 to 8 inches in length and is often present in large numbers.

This silver-scaled minnow often shows a purplish iridescent sheen along its sides, though its identification must be verified by a black mark at the base of the dorsal fin.

Like the trout with which the chub shares its home, it is fond of insects. Over half of its diet is insect life.

BLACKNOSE DACE—*Rhinichthys atratulus*

Another fish that likes clear-flowing brooks and streams to lakes and ponds is the 3-inch-long blacknose dace.

Though this little fellow's base color may vary from olive through brown and blue-black, a nose-to-tail black stripe accounts for its name. Spawning males get a reddish hue along the whole body.

Trout and bass fishermen often use this dace for bait as it is important in these fishes' daily diets. A feathered artificial bait

The blacknose dace actually is black from its nose to its tail.

is designed to look like the blacknose dace and goes by the same name.

COMMON SHINER—*Notropis cornutus*

This common minnow has probably been caught by every boy or girl who has ever dropped a line into the water. It lives in cold, clear brooks where it feeds on tiny insects that drift by or are discovered on the stream floor.

The common shiner does as its name suggests—shines.

The common shiner grows to about the same size as the creek chub but is not as "chubby." It is more flattened from side to side and a bit shinier in coloration—explaining where it got its name.

GOLDEN SHINER—*Notemigonus crysolencas*

The golden shiner gets its name from the golden hue on its sides.

Although it has about the same diet as the common shiner, in habitat and spawning methods it differs considerably.

Where the "common" is found in flowing waters, the "golden" is a fish of warm, weed-infested ponds, lakes, and slow-moving rivers.

Goldens built no nest but simply scatter their adhesive eggs in the shallows and abandon them. The male common shiner mates with the female in oxygen-rich riffles, then guards the nest for a time before leaving.

The golden shiner, along with other members of the family, including the fathead minnows, is raised commercially for bait and as food for hatchery bass and muskellunge.

The golden shiner is a popular bait fish.

11. *Fish that Live in Both Fresh and Salt Water*

Like birds, some fish migrate. No, they don't fly from one body of water to another, but they do have the unusual ability to live part of their lives in fresh water and part in salt water.

The reason for the migration is spawning. Some fishes, like salmon, striped bass, and shad, spend most of their lives in salt water then move into fresh water to spawn. These are known as *anadromous* (pronounced ah-nad'- drum-us) fish. Most migratory fish are anadromous.

The American eel is considered a *catadromous* (ka-tad'-drum-us) fish in that it matures in fresh water then moves to the ocean at spawning time.

SEA LAMPREY—*Petromyzon marinus*

Though they are frequently referred to as "lamprey eels," the lampreys are not in the same scientific grouping as the American eel or any of the other freshwater fish discussed in this book. In fact, they are among the most primitive of the higher animals and even more ancient than the sturgeon and paddlefish.

Ten species of American lampreys live in fresh water and four are anadromous. The best known of these, the sea lamprey,

The lamprey eels are among the most primitive of all fish-related animals.

inhabits the drainages of the Atlantic Ocean where it has become well known due to the destruction it has caused in recent years.

Back in the early 1920s, the sea lamprey was found to be present in Lake Erie. The lamprey had made its way from the Atlantic Ocean through the St. Lawrence Seaway and into not only Erie but the other Great Lakes as well.

Being a parasite, the lamprey needed a host on which to attach and draw nourishment. By attaching its suction mouth to a cod or haddock in the ocean, the lamprey could then suck the blood and body fluids of the fish with its rasplike teeth and tongue.

When it moved into fresh water, it had to find a new host. It found one in the lake trout. In fact, the millions of Great Lakes lampreys were so successful in finding trout that they practically eliminated the species from the lakes.

94

About 45 years ago, approximately 15 million pounds of lake trout were taken from lakes Huron, Superior, and Michigan each year.

Thirty years later the catch was reduced to less than a half-million pounds.

When the lake trout populations diminished, the adaptable lampreys turned to whitefish and ciscoes for their sustenance. It is believed that during their freshwater spawning times, a single lamprey may kill up to 40 pounds of fish.

The Atlantic sea lamprey grows to about 2½ feet. It is readily identified by a line of seven small round openings along each side of the body where gills would normally be found. These pores act as gills in respiration.

Shortly after spawning, both the male and female lampreys die. The eggs then hatch into larvae which burrow in the mud

These Great Lakes fish show lamprey scars.

of some calm water area. Here they remain for six or seven years, feeding on the microscopic drift of the stream.

The larval lampreys then develop eyes and toothed mouths and, in the spring, descend to the ocean to begin their parasitic lives.

Electric barriers, poisoning, and trapping have all been tried for lamprey control. Though these methods have met with moderate success, the lake trout that were once common in the Great Lakes will take many years to restore themselves to abundancy.

Of the fourteen species of lamprey in the United States, ten of them live strictly in fresh water and are not parasites.

The northern brook lamprey lives in the streams of eastern and midwestern America and grows only to about 6 inches.

The silver lamprey lives in the Great Lakes and is also a parasite like its larger, more common, and more destructive cousin. It averages less than a foot in length.

AMERICAN EEL—*Anguilla rostrata*

Unlike the lamprey, the American eel *is* a true fish, though it has no other family members living in North America's fresh waters.

The American eel is a true fish.

This eel is catadromous. It inhabits only the Atlantic Ocean and its tributaries. A close relative lives in Europe and uses the same spawning grounds as the American species.

Like the salmon, the eel returns to its birthplace to spawn and die. Unlike the salmon, though, the eel lives its adult life in fresh water then moves to salt water to spawn.

The spawning area is not just any part of the ocean but a specific spot between Bermuda and the Bahamas known as the Sargasso Sea.

During the late winter, the female eels lay 10 million or more eggs each in the depths of the calm, weed-infested Sargasso area. The adults then die. The eggs drift in the sea until finally hatching into half-inch, transparent, leaflike "leptocephali" (translated "thin heads").

During the following year the thin heads move toward American shores. By now they have grown to about 3 inches and, though still transparent, begin to resemble baby eels. Once they enter fresh water the young eels—now called "elvers"—take on a dark gray-green color.

In the bays and estuaries, the male and female elvers part company. The males will spend the next few years in the brackish water, while the females migrate inland to rivers, streams, and small brooks, sometimes for upward of a thousand miles, and grow to 3 feet in length. Here they remain for about eight or nine years.

When the reproductive urge strikes, the females move back into the bays where they meet younger males about half their size. They then mysteriously return to the Sargasso to continue the life cycles of their kind.

In some places, such as in Quebec, Canada, the eel is caught commercially for food. Many of these eels are sold to Italian families in the United States as a traditional food of the Christmas holiday season.

Strangely, the eel is a tough character and is known to make its way, in snakelike fashion, across wet fields and around dams to some pond or lake. Here they may become landlocked, never to complete their life cycles.

AMERICAN SHAD—*Alosa sapidissima*

The American shad's natural range is practically the entire Atlantic Coast from Canada to Florida. It is also present on the West Coast from Southern California to Alaska, where it was introduced over a century ago.

Like the famous salmon, the lesser-known shad has suffered because of pollution and the many river dams that prevent it from reaching its spawning grounds.

In the warmer southern states the large-scaled, silvery shad move into the bays and begin their upriver runs in January. Northward, the migrations are progressively later. Because many of these migratory trips are long (200 to 500 miles in some instances), the run may actually continue for several months until all of the fish reach suitable spawning grounds.

The shad actually begin their trips long before the water temperatures reach the 60 to 70 degrees F. range which stimu-

Lt. Governor Ernest Kline of Pennsylvania with an American shad caught in the Delaware River

Researchers from the U.S. Fish and Wildlife Service measure and tag a shad to study its migratory paths.

lates them to mate and shed their eggs. No nest is built, and the eggs are broadcast in fast-moving water and abandoned. The eggs drift with the current and hatch in about a week's time. The young grow to about 4 inches by fall, at which time they begin their downstream migration to the sea.

In some waters many of the young are faced with pollution which kills them. In the Delaware River, for example, a heavy area of pollution in the Trenton, New Jersey, and Philadelphia, Pennsylvania, area is critical. Most of the adult shad, which move downstream shortly after spawning, die in the polluted sector of the Delaware because of a lack of oxygen. Fortunately, by fall, higher waters and increased temperatures break up the pollution and many of the fry can get through safely.

The shad then live in the ocean for five or six years, at which time they mature sexually and return to fresh water once again.

Strangely, shad that spawn in the rivers from North Carolina south die after spawning—not from pollution but from natural causes like the salmon do.

Shad roe has always been a delicacy, and in years past millions of these fish were netted for their eggs and flesh.

Today the shad are prized by anglers who fish for them with lures known as "shad darts." Even though the fish are known not to feed during migration, they strike at the darts and can be caught by rod and reel. Scientists believe that the shad strike because of an instinctive desire to protect their spawning area from intrusion.

The American shad is a member of the herring family and two other relatives, the smaller gizzard shad (*Dorosoma cepedianum*) and the hickory shad (*Alosa mediocus*), inhabit many of the same waters.

PACIFIC SALMON

There are five species of Pacific salmon—all of the genus *Orcorhynchus*. These are:

Chinook salmon—*O. tshawytscha*
Coho salmon—*O. kisutch*
Sockeye salmon—*O. nerica*
Pink salmon—*O. gorbuscha*
Chum salmon—*O. keta*

Only the chinook and coho are important to sport fishermen, but the other three kinds are also taken in some waters.

Commercially, the pink salmon is the most important—this being the kind that can be bought canned from most grocery stores throughout the country.

At spawning time the silvery appearance of these salmon

100

Salmon leaping Kittiwake Falls near Brooks Lake, Katmai National Forest Monument, Alaska

changes to shades of yellow, red, and black. The males develop a hooked lower jaw.

All of the salmons move from the Pacific Ocean to spawn in fresh water. After a sometimes arduous task of migrating hundreds, or sometimes thousands, of miles upstream, the fish mate, spawn, and die. At this time they provide food for many varieties of wildlife such as gulls, eagles, and bears.

The young salmon hatch and remain in the gravel in which the eggs were laid until most of their yolk sac is used. They then emerge and begin to feed on plankton. The pink and chum salmon fry begin their downstream trips immediately, while the fall-hatched chinook lingers near its birthplace for three or four months. The coho, sockeye, and spring-hatched chinook may not begin their travels for a year or more.

The ocean life of each of the salmon varies from two to eight years, the sockeyes staying in salt water for the longest time. Here they feed on other fish, crustaceans, and squid.

One of the strangest behaviors of the salmon is their ability to return to the same waters in which they were hatched. Scientists have attempted to find out how these fishes can home in on their birthplaces, but most explanations are, at best, good guesses. One theory is that the salmons are able to detect the odors of certain rivers, but this may be only a small part of the mystery.

Over the years Pacific salmon, like so many other fish, have diminished in numbers through overfishing, destruction of habitat, pollution, and the construction of dams which stop the instinctive migratory movements.

CHINOOK SALMON

This is the largest of the Pacific salmon. A large fish weighs 60 pounds, though the average is only one-third this. There is a record of a 126-pound chinook.

This species is known to travel as much as 2,000 miles from the Pacific Ocean into the Yukon to spawn. It is the salmon most

A small chinook salmon caught in Lake Erie

sought after by sport anglers, and commercial fishermen also net them in large numbers while they are still in the ocean.

The chinook has also been stocked in the Great Lakes and is doing well despite the fact that it does not get as big as its West Coast relatives.

COHO SALMON

The coho is second to the chinook in numbers caught by anglers. Unlike its larger cousin, however, this "silver salmon" is content to spawn in streams close to the ocean.

The coho is silvery in color with black back spots. At maturity it weighs between 6 and 12 pounds.

Coho salmon range from California to Japan, though individual fish never travel far from the parent stream. Its chances for survival are bolstered by the fact that it does not need to travel great distances up rivers and streams which are often blocked by dams or poisoned by industrial pollutants.

Coho have been stocked in the Great Lakes where they have adapted well.

SOCKEYE SALMON

The sockeye is the most economically valuable of all the Pacific salmon. In 1961, almost $50 million worth of its flesh was sold to people across America.

Mature male sockeyes take a bright red coloration—outshining their drab olive-colored mates at spawning time.

Sockeyes are present from California to Japan, where they enter rivers fed by lakes to spawn. Spawning usually takes place in lakes or nearby in the inlet or outlet streams.

Some sockeyes spend their entire lives in fresh water, where they spawn and provide angling opportunity in areas where salmon are not normally found. These "landlocked" fish, called "kokanee salmon," never get as big as their saltwater relatives which average 6 pounds.

103

PINK SALMON

This is the smallest of the Pacific salmon, growing only to about 4 or 5 pounds at maturity.

At two years of age the males develop a hooked snout and a large hump on the back. They spawn in the fall, usually near the ocean but sometimes several hundred miles upstream.

The "pink" is the most abundant of the Pacific species and in some years accounts for nearly half of all canned salmon.

Scientists consider this fish to be the least dependent (of the five varieties) on fresh water and is even known to spawn in brackish water—where salt and fresh mix.

CHUM SALMON

Most chum salmon, unlike the other four species, possess no dark spots on the fins or body. Most noticeable, though, are the fish's large head, jaws, and teeth. Because of these features, it is sometimes referred to as the "dog salmon."

It ranges from California to the Arctic and is most abundant in the cold, northern waters.

The chum's average weight is about 10 to 12 pounds.

Strangely, this chum salmon is not considered a game fish because, like the pink salmon, it does not eat many fish and seldom is interested in a bait or lure.

ATLANTIC SALMON

ATLANTIC SALMON—*Salmo solar*

This entire book could be filled with information about the Atlantic salmon.

One of the most unique facts about this fish is that, unlike its Pacific counterparts, *Salmo solar* does not die after spawning. In fact, it often spawns more than once in its lifetime.

In the fall it comes to spawn, running the rivers of New-

This Atlantic salmon has been trapped for tagging and release for migration studies.

foundland, New Brunswick, Labrador, Nova Scotia, Quebec, and Maine. Across the sea it is also found in the waters of Greenland, Iceland, Norway, France, Germany, and Holland.

At one time the East Coast's Delaware and Hudson rivers laid claim to the Atlantic salmon.

Though it would seem that the Atlantic salmons' closest relatives are the Pacific salmons, such is not the case. The family that includes the brown, rainbow, and cutthroat trout are its next of kin.

Although Atlantic salmon of almost 80 pounds have been reported taken by rod and reel, the average is closer to 12 or 14. The salmon grows largest by living continuously in the sea. The spawning act inhibits growth because it is so rigorous. Biologists claim that, on any spawning run, only about 10 percent of the fish are return spawners. The other 90 percent are "maiden fish"—those making their first migratory trip.

After spawning, the adult "spent" salmon are usually sickly looking as they make their way back to the sea.

The eggs hatch and the young remain in fresh water for one to four years. During this time they are heavily preyed upon by birds and other predators. By the time the survivors are ready to make their seaward migration, they may still be only about 7 inches long. Three years later, when it returns to its birthplace to spawn, the same fish may weigh 20 pounds or more.

The Atlantic salmon is a highly prized catch of commercial net fishermen, as well as those using rod and reel. Many regulations cover both types of salmon harvests and fortunate is any angler who pulls a hefty 25-pounder from a fast-flowing river.

Like the American shad, the salmon does not feed on its spawning runs but is thought to strike a lure out of reflex rather than a desire to eat.

12. Other Interesting and Unusual Fish

Except for the minnows, none of the other chapters in this book deal with a scientific "fish family." Instead, the fish covered in each chapter share some ecological or behavioral characteristic—good fighters on a rod and reel, easy to catch and plentiful, ancient in structure, and so forth.

Many fish do not properly belong in any of these categories. The sucker, Johnny darter, sculpin, killifish, whitefish, and stickleback are just a few that deserve mention.

White sucker—*Catostomus commersoni*

Sixty-five species of suckers—the family Catostomidae—live across the United States. Of all these, the white sucker is most common.

The sucker could well be named "underwater vacuum cleaner"—both because of its unusual mouth and the method with which it feeds.

The sucker's mouth is a suction tube situated on the underside of the head. When feeding, it actually sucks small food items—worms, insect larvae, and vegetation—from the river or stream bottom in which it lives.

A young white sucker

Except for its mouth, the sucker could well be mistaken for a member of the minnow family—especially a carp or fallfish. Its colors are typically dull, though they do vary from olive-green through gray and bronze in various waters. The sucker's head has no scales, but the scales covering the rest of the body are quite large.

In the springtime, when the suckers move to shallow, gravel-bottomed water to spawn, they become the prime interest for many anglers who tend to ignore them at other seasons of the year.

During spawning two or three males may accompany a female, pressing against her as she sheds her eggs and they, their milt. Soon after the mating process the eggs are abandoned, and in less than two weeks swarms of sucker fry are seen swimming in the vicinity.

Because the sucker is very bony, it is not prized as table fare. In the spring, however, the flesh is sweet and tasty.

The sucker's average size is about 12 to 16 inches, but they will grow larger.

Though suckers are often accused of preying on the eggs of

game fish, scientists say this is not true. In fact, the many young suckers produced in the spring provide much food for the fish-eating predators with which they share a watery home.

JOHNNY DARTER—*Etheostoma nigrum*

A member of the family Percidae—the Johnny darter not only has an unusual name but it certainly is unusual itself when one considers that its close relatives include the yellow perch and walleye.

Ninety-five different species of tiny darters live in North America and are found nowhere else in the world. Some of them make up for their 1- to 3-inch sizes by exhibiting brilliant colors. The rainbow darter, also known as the "soldier fish," rivals the colors of any storebought aquarium fish.

"Johnny"—like all its midget-sized relatives—has no air bladder and spends most of its time on the stream bottom where it "darts" after minute crustaceans and insects.

This darter's main identifying feature is a scale pattern consisting of distinct V, X, and W markings along the sides.

In the spring the female darter deposits her eggs under stones where the male guards them. Although he is courageous, he

The Johnny darter is a close relative of the perch and walleye.

stands little chance against a large trout, and many darters serve as food for these larger predators.

Fly fishermen have even designed an artificial bait, called the "muddler minnow," to resemble the Johnny darter.

Mottled sculpin—*Cottus bairdi*

Most sculpins live in the ocean, though there are two that live in both fresh and salt water and eighteen that are full-time freshwater residents.

Like the darters, the less common sculpins prefer clear, cold-water lakes and streams. Here they are at their best in hiding their camouflaged bodies around and under small stones.

The mottled sculpin is scaleless and somewhat slimy. Its color is brownish with mottled patterns of dark brown and black.

One striking feature of this fish are the large pectoral fins, which it frequently props against rocks to aid in maintaining its place in fast waters.

The mottled sculpin has excellent camouflage protection and easily blends into its stony surroundings.

The brook stickleback is a real fighter at spawning time.

BROOK STICKLEBACK—*Eucalia inconstans*

This unusual little fish lives only in the streams east of Kansas. It gets its name from three to six spines in front of the dorsal fin.

The most unusual feature of the stickleback's life is its strange spawning ritual.

Each spring the male builds an elaborate nest from plant stems and other vegetation fastened by a sticky secretion from its kidneys.

The 2-inch fish then entices a female to the nest, where she lays her eggs. Other females may also lay their eggs in this same, tunnel-like structure.

When the females have done their duties, the spunky male drives them off, fertilizes the eggs, then stands guard like a "mother hen."

He stays on duty, fighting off any threat to the eggs or newly hatched fry. Sometimes he even builds two nests, spending equal time guarding both.

As the fry mature and begin to wander, the dutiful male may even capture them in his mouth and actually "spit" them back into the nest.

After a while, however, the job gets to be futile as the youngsters leave the nest area in increasing numbers.

LAKE WHITEFISH—*Coregonus clupea*

The lake whitefish is a natural associate of the lake trout, preferring similar water types and range. It is found throughout most of Canada and the northern United States.

When just caught, the whitefish is faintly bronze to green on the back with satiny-white sides. Its shape is compressed from side to side.

Though anglers frequently catch the whitefish, it is more important to commercial fishermen. They are smoked, then marketed throughout the world. Canada harvests about 20 million pounds of this species each year.

Though they do not resemble their family relatives—the salmons—in size or shape (the average is about 4 pounds), they do like the same clear, cold lakes and rivers.

Other species of whitefish include the round and mountain whitefish, the cisco, and the inconnu.

13. Endangered and Threatened
Freshwater Fish

Like so many birds, mammals, reptiles, and amphibians throughout the country, the fish, too, show up on our listings of "Endangered and Threatened Species."

An "endangered" species is one whose populations are dangerously low, and the probability of their becoming extinct in the foreseeable future exists.

An animal that is "threatened" is not in as much danger as an endangered species, but without aid from man their plights could easily become very serious.

In the mid-1970s the U.S. Fish and Wildlife Service listed thirty endangered fish species (or subspecies) and four threatened varieties of fish. Though none of them are as well known as the bald eagle or the grizzly bear, a few of the fish have gained publicity in various parts of the country.

The shortnose sturgeon, like others of its family, has been seriously harmed by overfishing in the past.

The Scioto madtom, a catfish, lives only in a small portion of Big Darby Creek, a tributary to Ohio's Scioto River. It is endangered because of pollution, siltation, and by two proposed dams on the river.

The snail darter

The snail darter, a 3-inch fish, was in the news frequently in 1977 when it helped environmentalists stop the building of a dam on the Little Tennessee River. Since the construction of the dam would have resulted in the extinction of this tiny fish, environmentalists were able to take their case to court under the Endangered and Threatened Species Act. Strangely, the snail darter lives in a 12-mile length of the river and feeds exclusively on snails.

The large cui-ui (pronounced "kee-wee"), which lives in Nevada's Pyramid Lake, and the Colorado River squawfish, (a large minnow that can grow up to 80 pounds), are victims of irrigation and dams.

Although there are a variety of reasons why certain species of fish are in trouble, siltation accounts for or contributes to most of them. As soil erodes from the land and washes into the waters it coats the stream bottoms, shuts out the sun so plants cannot grow, and affects the oxygen that a fish's gills can take in. Some biologists feel that siltation is the number one enemy of American freshwater fish.

In the past, it was overfishing that started many fish on their downhill paths. Now dams destroy habitats by making deep lakes of streams that once flowed over rocks and gravel. Irrigation removes millions of gallons of water from many midwestern rivers.

Then, of course, there are contributing factors such as pollution, dredging, draining, stream-straightening, and other practices that ruin fish habitat.

Following is a list of endangered fishes of the United States:

Shortnose sturgeon
Longjaw cisco
Greenback cutthroat trout
Gila trout
Humpback chub
Mojave chub
Pahranagat bonytail
Moapa dace
Woundfin
Colorado River squawfish
Kendall Warm Springs dace

Tecopa pupfish
Warm Springs pupfish
Owens River pupfish
Pahrump killifish
Big Bend gambusia
Unarmored threespine stickleback
Gila topminnow
Fountain darter
Watercress darter
Maryland darter
Blue pike

Colorado River squawfish

Cui-ui   Okaloose darter
Devil's Hole pupfish   Scioto madtom
Comanche Springs pupfish   Snail darter

These fishes are listed as "threatened" by the U.S. Fish and Wildlife Service:

Lahontan cutthroat trout   Arizona (Apache) trout
Paiute cutthroat trout   Bayou darter

Though few of these fishes are popular with fishermen, and many of them only dwell in small sections of the country, losing just one to extinction means that man has somehow failed as a custodian of his natural resources.

14. Create a "Window in a Pond"

Most aquarium hobbyists restrict themselves to gaudy tropical fish or fancy-finned species from the Far East. Yet many home aquariums contain fish which are every bit as interesting and colorful as the expensive foreign species . . . and they're virtually free for the taking. (It is suggested that the state law be checked first before taking any fish for your home tank.)

Setting up the native aquarium isn't much different than creating one for tropical fish. The main difference is that you've got to catch your stock in a pond or stream rather than buy them in a store. Of course, that's half the fun.

The way you choose to furnish and decorate your tank, and the foods you will be offering these natives, will vary somewhat from the tropical setup.

My own tank has been established for over two years and in that time I've discovered a few "musts" for raising native fish. In a nutshell, here are some requirements and suggestions for getting your own aquatic zoo in order:

1. Choose an aquarium and filter system to match. Since cleanliness is of utmost importance, the filter must be able to do an efficient job or the aquarium will soon become discolored and messy. Your local aquarium dealer should be consulted if there is any doubt as to your filter's potential. I've found the ex-

ternal, siphon-type filters with direct drive or magnet-driven motors to be quite satisfactory.

2. Although it's entirely a matter of personal taste, natural-looking aquarium gravel will give your native tank that realistic appearance. Though the brightly colored stones and novelty-type decorative items available at tropical fish stores have their purposes, they will not impart a natural appearance to your "pond."

I've also used stream floor gravel in some schoolroom aquariums with good results. This was thoroughly washed before use, however, to remove the fine sand and silt. If this is neglected, the particles will stay in constant suspension due to the action of the filter and the movements of the fish.

3. Set up your aquarium, including filter, gravel, and water, several days before you plan to introduce the fish. This will not

only give the gravel a chance to settle but the chlorine in the tap water will have a chance to evaporate. If pond water is to be used, it should first be boiled to kill any disease-producing organisms that might be in it.

4. If fish from a swift-flowing stream are to be "stocked" in your tank, an aerator should be used to supply sufficient oxygen. Most filters, however, will provide enough dissolved oxygen in a moderately stocked aquarium.

5. Decorative rocks and live plants may be added any time prior to the introduction of the fish. One or two large rocks (dependent upon your aquarium's size) should be gotten from a clean stream.

Although wild aquatic plants may be used, there is always the possibility of introducing a disease along with them. Since the fish are confined in closer quarters than they would be in the wild, diseases spread much more quickly and are sometimes fatal to the fish. "Ich" or "white spot disease" is a common malady of any captive fish. When this occurs, it is best to remove the infected individuals and treat the water with a "store-bought" medicine specifically concocted for such purposes.

6. Hardy, attractive aquatic plants are available from tropical fish shops. I'd suggest any combination of the following: *Cabomba* (fanwort), *Anacharis* (ditch moss), *Myriophyllum* (water milfoil), *Sagittaria* (arrowhead), *Vallisneria* (eel grass), and *Elodea* (waterweed). Living plants not only use the fertile wastes from the fish but supply oxygen as well.

7. The aquarium should be located so that the plants get about two hours of sunlight per day; otherwise they will not grow. Too much sunlight will cause a rapid growth of algae which coats the glass sides and makes the tank unattractive.

Tank location is not a problem if an artificial light is used. Since incandescent bulbs produce heat, flourescent types are best. The Grolux tube not only stimulates plant growth but gives the tank and its colorful residents a rich glow. Eight to ten hours of exposure per day is sufficient.

STOCKING THE TANK

Now that the tank is set up and furnished and the water has been "aged" for a few days, it's time to introduce the fish.

The species of native fish that will adapt to aquarium life is limitless. Although there's a tendency to want to keep larger individuals, bear in mind that crowding restricts freedom of movement. Therefore, I prefer to sacrifice fewer and larger fish for more of a variety of small ones. A good rule of thumb is not to have more than 1½ "inches of fish" for each gallon of water. A 30-gallon tank could conceivably provide space for as many as a dozen pairs of small fish. Some attractive species which do well in captivity are:

Blacknose dace	Yellow perch
Redbelly dace	White sucker
Redside dace	Johnny darter
Creek chub	Mottled Sculpin
Common shiner	Pumpkinseed
Emerald shiner	Bluegill
Stoneroller	Stickleback
Golden shiner	Brown bullhead
Madtom catfish	Fathead minnow

It is impossible on these pages to outline specific combinations that do well together in a community tank. Observe your fish closely during the first few days of captivity and remove the antagonists. Otherwise there will be many fish without tail fins.

You must also be careful to keep all fish about the same size. Don't try to add an 8-inch perch to a tank of small fish or soon you'll be without any small fish.

The addition of a few "nonfish" animals gives the native tank its finishing touches. Pond snails, small crayfish, small mussels,

Many communities and cities across the country have large aquariums open to the public. This sturgeon and crappie bass are just a few of many species on exhibit at the National Aquarium in Washington, D.C.

salamander larvae, newts, tadpoles, and even large aquatic insects are adaptable and extremely interesting.

Feeding time should occur only once a day. The tendency to overfeed is strong—but dangerous—due to the excess food decaying and thereby fouling the water. However, bullheads, crayfish, or other scavengers will often take care of any "leftovers."

Prepared fish food, dried shrimp, ground-up clams and oysters, and bits of beef liver should be alternated with live foods such as Tubifex worms (available at pet stores), Daphnia, and small earthworms.

Setting up and maintaining a healthy, well-balanced native aquarium demands time and effort. The rewards of having your own "window in a pond," however, will more than repay you and your family in education and enjoyment.

121

15. Fish for the Future

When Izaak Walton—the first man to write seriously about the joy and challenge of fishing—fished along the wilderness waters 300 years ago, he probably never dreamed that fish would be as dependent upon man as they are today.

Throughout this book there have been references to certain species of fish that have been transplanted in waters, often far from their original ranges, in which they would otherwise not live.

Throughout the years many species of fish have been transplanted to new waters. This is an old Pennsylvania Fish Commission hatchery operation showing how trout were transferred to open waters in milk cans.

Ichthyologists carry out endless studies on fish and fish habitats. Here they sample a lake to see what kinds and sizes of fish are present.

The American Fisheries Society was organized in 1870. Its members were made up of professional fishery workers and today it is one of the oldest scientific organizations in America.

The "fish facts" that these scientists gathered 50 and 100 years ago are no longer completely valid today. It is therefore necessary to continue an endless study of the three things on which successful fisheries are based: fish, environment, and people. All three must be considered if any fish management program is to be a success.

In recent years such organizations as the Bass Anglers Sportsman Society (BASS) and Trout Unlimited have been formed. These groups are composed of interested anglers who in turn support research on their favorite species.

Both federal and state-operated hatchery programs combine research and the production of both cold- and warm-water fish to stock the nation's waters.

As long as boys and girls and adults thrill to the tug of a sunfish on the end of a line, America's fishing future will be in good hands.

In recent years there has been an increased emphasis on restoring the runs of anadromous fishes—shad, salmon, striped bass, etc.—along both coasts. Untiring efforts are being undertaken to restore such waters as the Great Lakes, which were destroyed by the sea lamprey and pollution.

Throughout the country the increase in numbers of reservoirs, dams, and private ponds has created new fish habitats—each with potential for sport fishing and food.

But all of these efforts take money. At present, most of the management funds come from the sales of fishing licenses and taxes. Small private grants and donations also account for some local fishery projects.

No one really knows what the future holds. But as long as man shows concern for clean water and boys and girls thrill to the tug of sunfish at the ends of their lines, America's fishing future will be in good hands.

124

Bibliography

Burton, Maurice and Burton, Robert. *Encyclopedia of Fish*. Octopus Books, Ltd. (England). New York: Crown Publishers, 1975.

Curtis, Brian. *The Life Story of the Fish*. New York: Dover Publishers, 1949.

Eddy, Samuel. *How to Know the Freshwater Fishes*. Wm. C. Brown Co., 1969.

Fichter, George S. *Fishes*. New York: Golden Press, 1962.

La Gorce, John Oliver, ed. *The Book of Fishes*. Washington, D.C.: National Geographic Society, 1956.

McClane, A. J., ed. *McClane's Standard Fishing Encyclopedia*. New York: Holt, Rinehart, and Winston, 1965.

Trautman, Milton B. *The Fishes of Ohio*. Ohio State University Press, 1957.

Walden, Howard T., II. *Familiar Freshwater Fishes of America*. New York: Harper and Row, 1964.

Zim, Herbert S. and Shoemaker, Hurst. *Fishes*. New York: Golden Press, 1956.

Index

(Page numbers in **boldface** are those on which illustrations appear.)

128

DATE DUE

JUL 3 '79			
OCT 26 79			
DEC 13 '82			
MAY 29 '84			
AUG 22 '88	Al		
JUL 21 '94			
JUN 26 00			
GAYLORD			PRINTED IN U.S.A.